Tabo0
The world of
Forbidden

Zartashia Khanum

Contents

Introduction

It is very difficult to elaborate taboo in some extent. Taboos are varying culture to culture. Taboo is not entirely illogical or not befalls in abnormal behavior. Merely few are which I am going to bring out, some are interesting but some are absolutely lethal for humanity and never fit in modern scenario. According to general definition: A taboo is a fierce proscription of an activity firmly supported on the belief that such behavior is conversely too divine or too evil for ordinary individuals to undertake. Such prohibitions are present in virtually all societies. The word has been somewhat expanded in the social sciences to strong prohibitions relating to any area of human activity or custom that is sacred or forbidden based on moral judgment and religious beliefs. "Breaking a taboo" is usually considered objectionable by society in general, not merely a subset of a culture. Taboo: this word has forced me to go down to the depth of thought willingly. I looked around then dispersed society and realized that it is quite difficult to devise a specific definition of taboo. It is seems like as define normal and abnormal behavior because taboo behavior are also different from one culture or communities to other cultures or communities. According to my definition; A social or religious custom prohibiting or restricting a particular practice or forbidding association with a particular person, place or thing. I have a lot more questions and thoughts which are running through my head. What can we take meant of taboo? The behaviors that deviate from social or cultural norms are eligible to be called taboo. Merely I am not satisfied by this, sometimes things are going against social norms but it never befalls in taboo otherwise people who wear apron while bike riding must be labeled as taboo but it is not or in a drama character eating reddish with tea but we cannot call this a taboo behavior or we can call it? Do something different from social tradition have gotten the right to be called taboo? Does taboo categorized as a crime? Taboo is different than religious, social and moral norms. What could we call these things taboo on these grounds like intercourse with dead women, serial killing and marriage with holly book (Quran)?

The term "taboo" derives from the Tongan *tapu* or Fijian *tabu* ("impermissible", "banned", "forbidden"), related among others to

3

the Maori *tapu*, Hawaiian *kapu*, Malagasy *fady*. Its English use dates to 1777 when the British explorer James Cook visited Tonga, and referred to the Tongans' the term "taboo" used for "anything is not allowed to be eaten, or made use of". He wrote:

Not one of them would sit down, or eat a bit of anything. On expressing my surprise at this, they were all taboo, as they said; which word has a very comprehensive meaning; but, in general, signifies that a thing is forbidden.

The term was translated to him as "consecrated, inviolable, forbidden, unclean or cursed". *Tabu* itself has been derived from alleged Tongan morphemes *ta* ("mark") and *bu* ("especially"), but this may be a folk etymology (note that Tongan does not actually have a phoneme /b/), and *tapu* is usually treated as a unitary, non-compound word inherited from Proto-Polynesian **tapu*, in turn inherited from Proto-Oceanic **tabu*, with the reconstructed meaning "sacred, forbidden". In its current use on Tonga, the word *tapu* means "sacred" or "holy", often in the sense of being restricted or protected by custom or law. On the main island, the word is often appended to the end of "Tonga" as *Tongatapu*, here meaning "Sacred South" rather than "Forbidden South".

1

Sigmund Freud postulated that incest and patricide were the only two worldwide taboos and has given a shape the foundation of civilization. Despite anything to the contrary, whilst eating the flesh of own kind, in-group murder, and incest are taboo in the greater number of societies of societies, marriages amongst brothers and sisters came to pass in Roman Egypt.

usual taboos connect closely confinement or ritual regulation of killing and hunting; sex and sexual relationships for the most
part , necrophilia, miscegenation, pedophilia incest adultery, fornication,

intermarriage , bestiality, masturbation and homosexuality; reproduction abortion, infanticide; the dead and their graves; over and above food and dining primarily cannibalism and dietary laws such as vegetarianism, *kashrut*, and *halal* or religious haram. In Madagascar, a strong code of taboos, known as *fady*, perpetually modify and are formed from new experiences. Every area, village or tribe may have its own *fady*.

Taboos frequently broaden to address discussion of taboo topics just as cursing, resulting in genteelism and switch of words taboo. Occasionally the word "taboo" obtained widely popularity, with some scholars looking for ways to apply it where other English words had previously been applied. For example, J. M. Powis Smith, in his "The American Bible" (editor's preface 1927), used "taboo" occasionally in relation to Israel's Tabernacle and ceremonial laws, including Exodus 30:36, 29:37; Numbers 16:37,38; Deuteronomy 22:9, Isaiah 65:5, Ezekiel 44:19 and 46:20.

Theorists such as Communist and materialist have presented arguments that taboos can be utilized to uncover the histories of societies when other records are inadequate. Marvin Harris especially strived to explain taboos as a result of ecologic and economic conditions.

Psychology says new research out of Karolinska Institute's Emotion Lab in Sweden attempts to answer that question, by creating a psychological model behind the notion of tradition. It turns out that humans have a tendency to be quite sheep-like: the researchers found that it likely comes from a threat of punishment — as well as people's willingness to copy others.

"Critically, many social behaviors, such as cooperation and adherence to religious taboos, are maintained by threat of punishment," the authors wrote. "However, the psychological mechanisms allowing threat of punishment to generate such behaviors, even when actual punishment is rare or absent, are largely unknown.

In other words, people who adhere to tradition often due so for safety and survival. But people who see that tradition doesn't offer protection from danger are more likely to break out of it.

"We wanted to find out how these situations function in humans when we need to avoid danger," said Bjorn Lindström, a researcher at the Department of Clinical Neuroscience and an author of the study. "We discovered that two separate, simple, psychological mechanisms — the copying of others behavior and the rewarding properties of avoiding danger together forms a potent driving force that helps explain how we can create and maintain norms and traditions."

This is certainly a unique view of tradition. While not all traditions are bad — keeping your grandparents' ethnic rituals of holiday celebrations and language intact can maintain diversity in our world — some traditions can actually cause harm to humanity and go against basic human rights, according to Human Rights Watch.

"In countries around the world, Human Rights Watch has documented how discriminatory elements of traditions and customs have impeded, rather than Enhanced, people's social, political, civil, cultural, and economic writes," Graeme Reid writes.

Indeed, perhaps this research will offer a glimpse into what really creates tradition — and for us to better understand whether it offers genuine value to humanity or is only based in fear, punishment, and arbitrary taboos.

Source: Lindström B, Olsson A. Mechanisms of Social Avoidance Learning Can Explain the Emergence of Adaptive and Arbitrary Behavioral Traditions in Humans. (*Journal of Experimental Psychology*. 2015).

2

An overview of Asian culture and religious taboos

Taboos in Pakistani societies

In a day of shinny morning, I was sitting in my drawing room eating my meal. My elder aunt sitting along with me while eating we were discussing on different issues. Suddenly she asked me about marriage and started to scathing the scene how much I was going to be suffer if I never got marry. She said, if your parents will die how you could live alone. I smiled and said. I am strong and educated enough to handling my needs, marriage is nothing to do with it perhaps don't worry, I can search my partner to myself , my words hit her mind like a hammer, her green eyes got wide opened with wonder how shameless I was for her. Yes

Telling to someone about love and marriage is considered as a taboo behavior. Her ideas and reaction was taboo for me and mine was for her. But overall society has to have taboo behavior towards love marriages. Pakistani society has have more lethal taboos amongst other countries

Compare to other countries Pakistani society has had more lethal taboos.

3

Love marriages

Though it is a general perception in our society actual love begins after marriage. If a girl is to marry her 'boyfriend,' she's considered to be characterless (however it is shameful thoughts).

In conservative societies; where any girl who try to socialize with men, should be prepared to have questions raised about her character and moral boundaries.

Mostly parents discourage their children to choose a partner of their own choice, because They think that they put a lot of effort to raise their children so only parents have all right reserved to find a partner for their children (according to my point of view it's a kind of slavery). In that case if son choose a partner by his own family strongly dislike this behavior as well as girl too. The reason behind is that they at times are paranoid of an open minded girl who may not be keen to keep herself engaged with domestic chores. Girls who are not career-oriented and preferred to stay at home, considered the perfect daughter-in-law, from a lens of *mother in law*.

Another reason for such taboo is the fear of being killed, in the name of honor. Every other day news would flash on – that a mother, father, or brother murdered a women to save the families honor. Such cases are rife in rural areas where less education and glass ceiling of women is a tradition and those who attempt to break it face violent resistance.

Virginity

Living as they do in a conservative, Muslim-dominated society where pre-marital sex is a religious taboo, many Pakistani women are the prime victims of this religious taboo; after losing her virginity as well as for saving her life, and for wining husband's trust they go under the knife for hymen reconstruction surgeries to regain their lost virginity before marriage.

Take a glance on advertisements in English newspapers or websites or the walls of shops on busy street corners in cities, offering women a chance to enshroud their past by getting an artificial hymen - and you'll know

Enduring tradition holds that being a virgin is required for brides in Pakistan, and they are expected to prove it. It is still usual in some areas of the country for in-laws to check for blood stains the morning after a wedding as proof of the bride's virginity. The woman's own family is often behind the punishment, in some cases shunning the woman or handing her over to authorities for prosecution. But in the worst cases, victim's family members takeout honor killings. In some areas, women are killed for being not bleed at her first wedding night. In some cases, even after years of marriage, husband starts abuse his wife."

4

Let discuss some more hideous customs of Pakistan which are lethal for humans, especially for women.

Vani (custom)

Vani is a tradition that is found in certain region of Pakistan; wherein young girls are compulsorily married as part of punishment for a crime committed by her male relatives. It is a form of prearranged child marriage in which the resulting punishment is decided by a council of tribal elders named jirga. It is derived from Pashto word 'vanay' which means blood. Vani is also known as 'Sak', 'Swara' and 'Sangchatti' in different regional languages of Pakistan. Vani can be avoided if the kin of the girl agrees to pay money, called Deet.

This custom is said to have been started almost 400 years ago when two Pashtun tribes in north western Pakistan fought a bloody war against each other. During this bloody period around 800 people were murdered. The local chief tried to resolve this tension by calling the 'Jirga' who decided that girls are to be given as 'Qisas', as punishment. They considered it the only way to resolve this dispute and both families turned into a 'Birad'. Later on this decision became a custom which was passed on from generation to generation. Since then, tribal and rural jirgas have been using young virgin girls aged 4 to 14 to settle crimes such as murder by men. This blood for blood tradition can be found in different provinces of Pakistan such as KPK, Punjab, Sindh, Balochistan, as well as in the tribal areas. The practice has no legal or religious basis and constitutes an ancient tradition that is extensively customary in tribal and rural areas.

A terrible incident appear briefly on national and international media a few years back when eight innocent girls were married as 'Vani' in Mianwali; one of them was just one and a half year old. Various human rights organizations are working to root out this inhuman and stupid custom which is creating serious disorder in the society and destroying women's lives. Pakistan has already been facing severe reprimand for human rights violations and the incidents of vani bring huge shame to Pakistan.

Usually 'Vani' is applied in the cases of murder and kidnapping of womenfolk. When a jirga is called upon to resolve a case of murder or kidnapping of a girl, the jirga indicts the offender and announces punishment. In a murder case, punishments are either revenge i.e. blood for blood or blood money or 'Vani'.

In 2011, a 12 year old girl was handed over as wife to an 85 year old man under 'Vani' for a crime alleged to have been committed by the girl's father. In Malahanwala, Hafizabad, a 10 year old girl was forcibly married to a 50 year old man under the vani custom to compensate for her father's second marriage in the district. In 2012, 13 girls ranging from age 4 to 16 years were forced into marriage to resolve a dispute over a contention of murder between two clans. The case was tried by elders from the two groups with a member of Balochistan state assembly, Mir Tariq Masoori Bugti, who was leading the jirga. The jirga's verdict was based on 'Vani' enacting an order that the 13 girls must be handed over as wives to members of one of the clans, for a crime committed by a man of the other clan, who could not even be found for the trial. The sentence was carried out, and the politician Mr. Bugti fortified the practice of 'Vani' as a valid means to reconcile disputes.

5

Honor killings (karo kari)

Pakistan is an under developing country. More than half of its population lives in a typical traditional rural areas. Social norms and cultural values are deeply rooted here. It is largely practiced in tribal areas of Sindh. Therefore, the concept of killing a woman on the name of honour is a part of tribal culture. It is the social, economic and political brocade of our society. The paper chalks out the role required by law makers, law enforcement agencies, civil society organizations and community for stopping cruel culture of female victimizing and restoring the assumed notions of honour. The study has highlighted the main and important reasons and factors of honour killings in Sindh. Honour killing is not only limited to karo-kari, it has many other forms. are known locally as *karo-kari* . An honour killing is the homicide of a member of a family or social group by other members, due to the belief the victim has brought dishonour upon the family or community. The death of the victim is viewed as a way to restore the reputation and honour of the family.

Originally, karo and kari were metaphoric terms for adulterer and adulteress, but it has come to be used with regards to multiple forms of perceived immoral behavior. Once a woman is labeled as a kari, family members consider themselves to be authorized to kill her and the co-accused karo in order to restore family honour. In the majority of cases, the victim of the attacks is female with her attackers being male members of her family or community. This is conversation between I and the eye witness of such type of cases of honor killing.

I have discussed regarding this matter with a person who was eyewitness.

He told me

Yes i am an eye witness to many such events. Always the weak gender has been subjected to the so called justice and many times the other party went out unhurt.

Case#01: The accused girl was given the choice of a Bullet or Poison. She accepted poison. Her age was 09 years at that time. The boy fled to Malaysa

Case#02: The brother asked the accused sister, how to execute her. she opted to die when in prostration (Sajdah). the brother killed her inn prostration at her own request. The man is still dwelling n the area.

In both cases the girls were 100% innocents.

There are many other such events not mere stories, where i have been physically present to see the situation unfolding.

There are a lot more cases of honor killing.

Who can forget the latest tragedy of social media celebrity of Qandeel Baloch. Qandeel Baloch was a Pakistani model, actress, feminist activist and social media celebrity. Baloch rose to prominence due to her videos on social networks discussing her daily routine and various controversial issues. She was famous for her sensational videos on social media. Baloch first received recognition from the media in 2013, when she auditioned for *Pakistan Idol*; her audition went viral and she became an Internet celebrity. She was one of the top 10 most searched for persons on the internet in Pakistan and both celebrated and criticized for the content of her videos and posts. During the evening of 15 July 2016, Baloch was asphyxiated while she was asleep in the house where her parents live in Multan. Her brother confessed to the murder saying she was "bringing disrepute" to the "family's honour".

Dowry
Pakistan is a male dominant society and to fulfill the religious obligation "Marriage", the burden is bear more of the woman family. Marriage strengthens the relation not just to two people but between two families. However, dowry is a cultural taboo which weakens the relationship. It is a compensation given by the Bride's parents to the Groom family. It can be in any form cash, furniture, household items or vehicle.

It is common, especially in the modern era. There are many NGO`s who are taking radical steps to eliminate this exercise. They are working to protect the women rights and fighting against Dowry system. The most unethical and dreadful action is dowry. It is common against uneducated and illiterate people but still you will observe the educated people fulfilling it with pride.

According to the 1999 report, the cases of burning bride reached to 60 in 5 years. Dowry has gained the status and symbol in our society.

Divorce

Many couples have to face abusive married life. The people of our society recommend the woman, especially wife to cooperative and bear the violence and infidelity because of IZZAT. However, there is no such IZZAT in living a miserable life. Divorcees are looked down upon and are known as failures. It is reflected as a shameful act and people judge him/her by character.

Transgender in our society are more associated with prostitution and begging. It is very inhumane to live in a society where some people do not consider you human. Trans community has to face every sort of discrimination, and this is the reason they have to bear unwelcoming eyes.

WATTA SATTA

Is also a cultural Taboo which means give-take. It is very common practice in Pakistan and less advanced countries. It is a simultaneous marriage which occurs in the pair form such as brother- sister pair from two houses. It involves the pairs of uncle-niece or usually cousin. 90 percent of WATTA SATTA marriages happen within the same caste or creed.

Families perform and establish it as a shadow of a mutual threat. If a husband mistreats his wife, then the brother in law will take revenge from his wife. It is cited as a little domestic violence.

6

Religious practices

Superstition in Pakistan is widespread and many adverse events are attributed to the supernatural effect. Superstition is a belief in supernatural causality: that one event leads to the cause of another without any physical process linking the two events, such as astrology, omens, witchcraft, etc., that contradicts natural. In Pakistan, the Magical thinking pervades as many acts and events are attributed to supernatural and ritual, such as prayer, sacrifice, or the observance of

a taboo are followed. Many believe that magic as it has placebo
effect to psychosomatic diseases. Scholars of Islam view superstition as shirk,
denying the unity of God and against Sharia. Within Islam, shirk is
an unforgivable crime; God may forgive any sin if one dies in that state except for
committing shirk. Sleeping on your right side and reciting the Ayat-ul-Kursi of
the Quran can protect person from the evil.

In Pakistan, mental illness and psychological problems are considered by some to
be an encounter with Shaitan(Satan) evil jinns or demons who have taken over
one's body and mind. It is also assumed that it is caused by the black
magic performed by enemies and jealous persons. People, especially children and
young girls, wear Ta'wiz (Amulet) to   ward off evil
eye. Spells, incantations and curses could also result
in ghouls or churail(witch) haunting a person. Some homes and places are also
believed to be haunted by evil ghosts (Bhoot), satanic or other supernatural beings
and they could haunt people living there especially during the night. Muslim holy
persons (Imams, Maulvis, Sufis, Mullahs, Faqirs) perform exorcism on individuals
who are believed to be possessed. The homes, houses, buildings and grounds
are blessed and consecrated by Mullahs or Imams by
reciting Qur'an and Adhan the Islamic call to prayer, recited by the muezzin.
In Pakistan, Sleep paralysis is considered to be an encounter
with Shaitan (Satan), evil jinns or demons who have taken over one's body.
This ghoul is known as 'bakhtak' or ifrit

The penchant for faith healers and black magicians spans Pakistani society, from
the rich landlords of the rural areas to the urban classes of Lahore and Karachi. The
villagers of Rajanpur rural Punjab, call upon a Pir believed to be endowed
with mystical powers that can purify contaminated water after severe floods.
Pakistanis from all walks of life routinely turn to faith healers to remedy
various health problems, from Abdominal pain to Epilepsy,
avert marriage meltdowns and financial crises and even fend off the powers of
other healers.

Many in Pakistan believe that black magic or sorcery can help reduce their
problems, cure diseases, or even bring good luck. Such practices are common not

only in the far-flung rural areas, where many of people low education, but also in big cities with higher education like in Islamabad, Faisalabad and Karachi

Human bones in occult

There are grave-digging incidents in Karachi and cemeteries in different regions of Pakistan where bones are stolen from the graves. The two suspects, who had been caught and arrested they denied involvement in digging up graves to

steal human bones for use in black magic, which many believe is a booming business in the country, particularly in rural areas. Occult practices are believed to be widespread in Pakistan where religious beliefs, superstitions and illiteracy play a big role in everyday life. A recent grave-digging incident in Karachi has highlighted this.

Former president

The former President Asif Ali Zardari was obsessed with the occult and the superstition. According to the media reports, "A black goat is slaughtered almost daily to ward off `evil eye` and protect President Asif Ali Zardari from `black magic`," says Pakistan's leading newspaper Dawn. "It has been an old practice of Zardari to offerSadaqah (charity) of Animal sacrifice and distribute meat to the poor.[4] He has been doing this for a long time," the newspaper quoted the Pakistan president's spokesman Farhatullah Babar as saying.

Mourning of Muharram

The Mourning of Muharram, Remembrance of Muharram, or Muharram Observances, is a set of rituals associated with both Shia and Sunni, which takes place in Muharram, the first month of the Islamic calendar. Many of the events associated with the ritual take place in congregation halls known as *Hussainia*.

The event marks the anniversary of the Battle of Karbala when Imam Hussein ibn Ali, the grandson of Muhammad, was killed by the forces of the second Umayyad caliph Yazid I at Karbala. Family members, accompanying Hussein ibn Ali, were killed or subjected to humiliation. The commemoration of the event during yearly mourning season, from first of Muharram to twentieth of Safar with Ashura comprising the focal date, serves to define Shia communal identity. At present, Muharram observances are carried out in countries with a sizable Shia population.

Zanjeer zani

Tatbir (Arabic) is amongst a set of bloody rituals that are performed by some Shia Muslims in commemoration of the great tragedy of Karbala, when the family of the Holy Prophet Muhammad (s) was massacred by a group of Muslims. Tatbir is performed by striking the head with a sword or knife until blood gushes out. In the Persian language Tatbir is called Qama Zani.

Some Shias in the Indian subcontinent also perform an act called Zanjeer Zani (usually called Zanjeer). It involves repeatedly striking the back with a chain of blades with the intention of cutting the skin and causing blood to flow. Tatbir and Zanjeer are the two most widely practiced of the blood shedding rituals. Other rituals include injuring oneself with a stone, padlock or chain.

7

Blasphemy

The Pakistan Penal Code prohibits blasphemy against any recognized religion, providing penalties ranging from a fine to death. From 1987 to 2014 over 1300 people have been accused of blasphemy, Muslims constitute the majority of those booked under these laws.

Over 60 people accused of blasphemy have been murdered before their respective trials were over, and prominent figures who opposed the blasphemy law have been assassinated. Since 1990, 62 people have been murdered as a result of blasphemy allegations.

According to one religious minority source, an accusation of blasphemy commonly subjects the accused, police, lawyers, and judges to harassment, threats, attacks and rioting. Critics complain that Pakistan's blasphemy law "is overwhelmingly being used to persecute religious minorities and settle personal vendettas," but calls for change in the blasphemy laws have been strongly resisted by Islamic parties - most prominently the Barelvi school of Islam.

Pakistan's laws became particularly severe between 1980 and 1986, when a number of clauses were added to the laws by the military government of General Zia-ul Haq, to "Islamicise" the laws and deny the Muslim character of the Ahmadi minority. Prior to 1986, only 14 cases pertaining to blasphemy were reported.

Cases under blasphemy law have also been registered against Muslims who have harassed Non Muslims.

Asiyah bibi is a Pakistani Christian woman who was convicted of blasphemy by a Pakistani court, receiving a sentence of death by hanging. In June 2009, Noreen was involved in an argument with a group of Muslim women with whom she had been harvesting berries after the other women grew angry with her for drinking the same water as them. She was subsequently accused of insulting the Islamic prophet Muhammad, a charge she denies, and was arrested and imprisoned. In November 2010, a Sheikhupura judge sentenced her to death. If executed, Noreen would be the first woman in Pakistan to be lawfully killed for blasphemy.

The verdict, which was reached in a district court and would need to be upheld by a superior court, has received worldwide attention. Various petitions, including one that received 400,000 signatures, were organized to protest Noreen's imprisonment, and Pope Benedict XVI publicly called for the charges against her to be dismissed. She received less sympathy from her neighbors and Islamic religious leaders in the country, some of whom adamantly called for her to be executed. Christian minorities minister Shahbaz Bhatti and Muslim politician Salmaan Taseer were both assassinated for advocating on her behalf and opposing the blasphemy laws.[5] Noreen's family went into hiding after receiving death threats, some of which threatened to kill Asia if released from prison

Untold stories of blasphemy

Hafeez was born in Rajanpur and attended King Edward Medical College in Lahore, Pakistan after being given a gold medal in pre-medical studies at the Board of Intermediate and Secondary Education in the Dera Ghazi Khan division. In 2006 he left his medical studies to focus on English Literature at Bahauddin Zakariya University in Multan. In 2009 he travelled to Jackson, Mississippi to continue his studies at Jackson State University where he majored in American literature, photography and theater. He returned to BZU Multan in 2011 as a graduate student and a visiting lecturer for the English Department while also teaching at the College of Design. Soon after his arrival he faced broad disapproval from the Islamist group Jamaat-e-Islaami and its fellow group Tehrik-tahafaaz-e-Namoos-e-risalat. On March 13, 2013 a group of students started distributing pamphlet calling arrest of Junaid Hafeez. They soon staged a strike involving about some 1500 students from English and different other departments and Hafeez was expelled from the university and his contract was rescinded. Hafeez was soon arrested and held at Sahiwal Jail on the charge of violating section 295-C of the Pakistan Penal Code which held that if you in any way "defile" the name of Muhammad you "shall be punished with death".

He was accused of using the account Mulla Munnafiq to comment about Muhammad's wives in the closed group of "Liberals of Pakistan." The police claim to have gathered 1200 pages of material that incriminates him from his computer as well as a book called "Progressive Muslims" that he had received. Hafeez has faced a hard time finding a lawyer to defend him as the public in Pakistan views negatively anyone who defends someone accused of blasphemy. His original lawyer Mudassar left the case in June 2013 after facing a multitude of death threats.

Rashid Rehman then took on the case. Facing a multitude of death threats himself, Rehman commented to BBC that it was like "walking into the jaws of death" to defend someone accused of blasphemy in Pakistan. A hearing for Hafeez was held on April 3, 2014 at Multan Central Jail and Rehman was told that he would not live to attend the next hearing by the prosecuting attorneys. Despite these threats being made in front of the presiding Judge no charges were brought against them. On May 7, two men walked into Rehman's office in Multan and shot him to death before leaving the scene. The crime remains unsolved as of November 15, 2014.

Hafeez is represented by Shahbaz Gurmani as of December 2014; Gurmani has also received death threats including an incident where guns were fired outside of his home. Shahbaz Ali Khan Gurmani known as Shahbaz Gurmani is also the lawyer of other blasphemy accused persons. He is working on the Plat form of New Vision Foundation, Multan for the protection of Human Rights

The Lahore High Court has admitted the appeal of Dr. Sheikh, Pakistani rationalist and founder president of "The Enlightenment", against the death sentence awarded to him for blasphemy by the Islamabad additional district and session court on 18 August (Saturday). Dr. Sheikh was given only one week's time to appeal in the High Court.

The sister of Dr Sheikh made the appeal on 21 August (Tuesday) on behalf of him. A court official has confirmed that the appeal had been admitted.

Dr. Muhammad Younus Sheikh, British educated physician and physiology professor in a local medical college was arrested on 4 October 2000 by the Islamabad police and booked under Section 295 C of the Pakistan Penal Code.

Dr. Shaikh was accused to have defied Prophet Muhammad with his statement that Muhammed did not become a Muslim before the age of forty and that his parents were non-Muslims. Dr. Shaikh was found guilty and convicted under the law that prescribes death sentence if charges of blasphemy are proved. This law was added to the Pakistan Penal Code in 1986 which said whoever made derogatory remarks about Prophet Muhammed "by words either spoken, or written, or by visible representation or by any imputation, innuendo or insinuation, directly or indirectly, defiles the sacred name of Holy Prophet Muhammed (PBUH), shall be punished with death or imprisonment for life, and shall also be liable to fine.

Atheism

Pakistan is the land of the intolerant. People here have one belief: that their version of religion is the only right one. We frequently indulge in 'discussions' with our friends/relatives/just-about-anyone about the 'right' way to pray, the 'right' time to open your fast or the 'right' way to do *wudu* etc. We're obsessed with finding the 'right' way to do things. And once we know it, we make it our duty to tell anyone who'd listen's

In a land where having a different interpretation of one *ayah* of the Quran can get you murdered by your own guard, imagine the lives of those who've dared to challenge the norms and declared themselves apostates.

The topic of atheism is taboo in Pakistan. We don't talk about it, we don't think about and we don't write articles about it. Yet, this small minority continues to grow. Behind pseudonyms and fake Facebook profiles exist a large number of ex-Muslims in Pakistan. Kids raised in Muslim homes, grown up to abandon the faith. The annual "freedom of thought" report from the International Humanist and Ethical Union, an advocacy umbrella group that represents and seeks to protect non-religious people, details laws and practices around the world that punish or restrict atheism. The group presented the report to the United Nations today.

The report tracks, among other things, which countries have laws explicitly targeting atheists. There are not many, but the states that forbid non-religiousness – typically as part of "anti-blasphemy" legislation – include seven nations where atheism is punishable by death. All seven establish Islam as the state religion. Though that list includes some dictatorships, the country that appears to most frequently condemn atheists to death for their beliefs is actually a democracy, if a frail one: Pakistan. Others include Saudi Arabia, Iran, Afghanistan, Sudan, the West African state of Mauritania, and the Maldives, an island nation in the Indian Ocean. These countries are colored red on the above map.

For anyone who is not aware, the most dangerous minority to be in Pakistan is not (contrary to popular belief) an Ahmadi, but an atheist, a disbeliever in any form of God(s); an apostate and therefore, directly *wajibul qatl*. While there may still be some room for debate about the discriminatory mention of Ahmadis in Pakistan's constitution, so great is the taboo of atheism that it cannot even be whispered in close quarters with friends and family, let alone in parliament, the courts or the broader media sphere.

8

Home cleaning In conservative societies of Pakistan at evening is ominous. It is linked to disaster e.g. death of family members or devastating disease. This indicates Pakistan is dogmatic country they believe to follow their ancestors because they were on right path and have accurate knowledge about good and evil. In many areas when someone from home goes on journey it is menacing to sweep. It could bring calamity of a traveler.

Mental illnesses have long been avoided in our society. People are scared to go to psychologists they're wrongly associated with madness, regardless of how small or severe the illness might be. The way our society sees it, a man showing signs of depression or anxiety is termed to be weak or feminine (since we're all a bunch of sexists, too) and a woman seeking medical help for the same is considered unfit for marriage (because obviously, women are being prepped like goats for slaughter and this is all they're good for, enforcing the aforementioned sexism straight up psychotic or seeking attention.

A society where someone trying to seek therapy is termed *pagal,* ridiculed and made a joke of is a society that urgently requires a broader perspective. Mental health is directly linked to one's well being and it's about damn time that we give it the importance it deserves. And, to anyone who has depression, anxiety or any other mental illness, stay strong and keep fighting.

Holy months:
The word "Muharram" means "Forbidden." Even before Islam, this month was always known as a scared month in which all unlawful acts were forbidden, prominently the shedding of blood. There are many bounties of this month, especially on 10th of Muharram.10th of Muharram: On this day he who spends more lavishly for the sake of his family members, Allah Ta'aalaa will bestow

blessing upon the sustenance of the following year. Qiyaamah(judgment day) will take place on the 10th of Muharram.

Means Rajaba "to respect". Another one of the sacred months in which fighting was forbidden prior to Islam. This was one of the most respected months for the Arabs. It is also called Rajab al Fard. Fard means alone; because the other three sacred months come one after another, except this month. It comes alone not like the other 3 consecutive sacred months. The Holy Prophet Mohammed ascended to Heaven on the 27th of Rajab on either Sunday or Monday (Mi'raaj).

Meaning: Taken from the word "qa'ada" which means to sit. This is the third sacred month in which fighting was forbidden. The people also used to stop their business activities during this month and sit and prepare for the Hajj (Pilgrimage). This is also a sacred month.

Meaning: The month of "Hajj" (Pilgrimage). This is the last sacred month in which fighting was forbidden. The fifth pillar of Islam "Hajj" is performed in this sacred month. The first ten days of Zul-Hijjah are the most virtuous days in this whole month; Hajj is performed amongst these ten days.

Hardhat Abu Haraira (R.A) reports from the Holy Prophet : "Amongst all days there are none better to engage in sole worship of Allah than in the ten days of Zul-Hijjah, To observe a fast on any of these days is equivalent to fasting throughout the year, to actively engage in prayer and worship throughout any of these nights holds such rewarding values leveling with "night of power" (Laylatul-Qadr) "Tirmizi"

It has been stated in the Holy Qur'an, "By the dawn; By the ten nights (ie. the first ten days of the month of Zul-Hijjah), and by the even and the odd (of all the creations of Allah) and by night when it departs. There is indeed in them (the above oaths) sufficient proofs for men of understanding. (and that they should avoid all kinds of sins and disbelief)"
Hadhrat Abi Qataadah (R.A) reports in a part narration from the Holy Prophet concerning the fast observed on the day of Arafaat: "I have full

confidence in Allah for the one who observes a fast on the day of Arafaat that his previous year's sins and the proceeding year's sins are forgiven."(Muslim)

Eid ul Adha is one of the prestigious festivals of the Islamic calendar. Eid ul Adha is marked as the end of the Hajj, where the Muslims perform the obligation of Hajj, goes to the point to making the sacrifice of the animals which is the Sunnah of Prophet Ibrahim AS. Eid Ul Adha is popularly signified as the Festival of Sacrifice. The incident of Hazrat Ibrahim, who saw a dream that Allah has asked him to make a sacrifice of his son to Him. In order to raise the foundations of Kabbah, black stone and Muslim shrines in Madinah. Without raising any further questions, he responded to Allah's orders and asked his son Hazrat Ismael AS to come along in Makkah for the sacrifice. As soon Hazrat Ismael was told about the dream, he agreed to his father without any question and become submissive to carry out the commands of Allah. Hazrat Ismael was brave enough to give his life for Allah. Well, Allah is the most merciful and loving, was pleased with the Hazrat Ibrahim AS and Ismael AS intentions of sacrifice and a miracle happened. Instead of Hazrat Ismail, a lamb was replaced by the boy's life. Thus, Hazrat Ibrahim sacrificed the lamb ultimately. The number of animals slaughtered every year during the holy month.

DNA test, ,

CII members declared the cloning process 'Haram' or 'forbidden' under Islam, saying it would not be permitted. The Council of Islamic Ideology rejects DNA testing as primary evidence because it isn't mentioned in the Qur'an. The Qur'an mandates that four witnesses are required to establish sexual crimes — *zina* — and that's that. Women are victimized by this ridiculous and impossible rule? Who cares? It's the will of Allah.

Necrophilia

In Karachi, a man stood tall at five foot five inches with a white cloth covering his face at the North Nazimabad police station. DSP allege that accused has admitted to having profaned the corpses of 48 women in the Paposh Nagar graveyard for the past eight years.

"We had had vague understanding that something fishy was going on in the cemetery but we did not know what was wrong," he said. "We had gotten some of the gorkans [grave diggers] to work with us and keep an eye on this man for a month." The DSP added that accused could not have been caught earlier as he had vanished into thin air.

While talking to the media on Saturday, accused said that he had heard about a new grave of woman had been dug. "I went inside the grave as I usually do and got terrified," he said. "The dead woman's face and teeth were skanky. There was a light in her eyes that really horrified me. I got away as fast as I could and started running." He added that when he saw the dead woman's face, he had sworn never to indulge in these sort of activities ever again.

As accused started running away from the grave in fear, he caught the attention of grave diggers and other people. Soon there was a mob running after him with sticks and stones. Everyone, including the police thought that he was a thief or murderer. "We were conducting a snap check in the area when we found out," said the police. "We thought the people had caught a robber or something, had no idea that it would be something so strange." They claim that by the time they had figured out what accused did, the mob was ready to beat him up and tear him to pieces. They took him to the North Nazimabad police station for further investigations. Accused claims that his family is from Sargodha but he has spent his whole life in Karachi. He joined the graveyard about eight years ago to water the plants and graves. "I got a job through one of the grave digger." Accuser's crime used to go undetected as the graves were 'katcha' or the earth was freshly dug.

(Published in The Express Tribune, October 30th, 2011).

Chinese Taboos

Some interesting facts about Chinese taboos, When in Rome, do as Romans do."

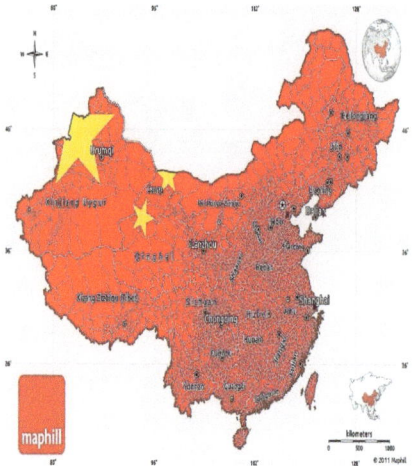

And when in China, do as Chinese people do. When you are learning Chinese, you need to know taboos in China. In Chinese culture, there are umpteen taboos that you never like to attempt, for the reason they may take BAD luck.

Use Chopsticks Correctly Dining at a Chinese table, you need to be careful don't leave chopsticks standing straight up in the bowl of rice. This is perceived as bad dining etiquettes. According to Chinese taboo, this act is said to bring bad luck as the chopsticks in rice look similar to the tombstone in the graveyard. So, just put them down on the table when you are not using them.

Giving the Right Gifts

Chinese is a nation that emphasizes on exchanging gifts. By giving gifts, the relationships are enhanced. However, you cannot give a Chinese friend these gifts: You should never give 钟 clock as a gift. 钟(zhōng) is a homophone of 终(zhōng), which means "the end". And the phrase 送钟 sòng zhōng (to give a clock) has the meaning of 送终(sòng zhōng), which means to farewell a person who is dying. Similarly, you should not give 伞(sǎn) which pronounces similar to 散(sàn), meaning "to go separate ways".

Taboo in China regarding green hat, you may have seen a green T-shirt, a green bag, or green shoes, but never a green hat! This is because no one wants to wear a Green Hat! In China, wearing a green hat means to cheat on your husband. There are many versions of stories about this saying. One of them is that the wife made a green hat for her husband, so each time the husband wearing the green hat walks back home, the wife and her lover can see it from far distance and have time to let her lover leave before the husband notice anything.

Don't Share a Pear
Sharing a pear with your friends or families, especially your loved ones can be a big taboo in China. In Chinese, the phrase for "sharing a pear" is 分梨(fēn lí). It is a homophone of 分离(fēn lí) which means "to separate". Certainly you don't want to separate with your loved ones. So, whenever you eat a pear, eat it all by yourself!

Don't Cut Hair in the First Month of the Lunar Year
According to Chinese culture and traditions, cutting your hair in the first month of the lunar year can bring very bad luck to your 舅舅(jiù jiu), who is your mother's brother or uncle in English. To perform best practices and to bring good luck in the coming New Year, one should not cut hair until Feb 2nd in Chinese lunar calendar.

Don't cry on New Year's Day
Chinese New Year is the most important festival in China. There are many traditions on this day such as exchanging Chinese New Year greetings, setting firecrackers, etc. Because it is the new beginning, Chinese people will make this festival "perfect" and avoid any unhappy things including CRYING. If you do cry, it is said you will cry all year.

Get Away from Four
Chinese people specially don't like the number 4(sì), because it is a homophone of the Chinese character 死(sǐ), which means "to die" in Chinese. That's why in China you see the English letter "F" instead of 4 in the elevators. In another case

when you bargain in China, avoid the price that contains the number 4 in it, such as 14, 144, etc.

Don't Whistle at Night

You must keep away from whistling during the night. In China, people believe spirits and ghosts will come out at night to perform daily activities. According to the old individuals, whistling at night is certain to draw the attention of wandering spirits who will follow the whistle and take away the person who whistles. Sound scary, right?

Indian taboos

In India there are so many ideas or beliefs that are taboos and a big hindrance in progress of Indian society. Somehow, Pakistan and India have some similar taboos. The most common taboos are in Indian society:

Speaking about sex in public is bad, it is not to be discussed, and doing anything that is even remotely sexual like masturbating is a crime. People also shy away from using birth control pills or condoms because going and asking for such things means that you are indulged in sexual activities.

Talking about menstruation in public is wrong, it is definitely not a part of Indian culture and people who do it are not well-cultured or rooted. A girl undergoing menstruation is unclean, and thus should not be allowed to pray or do certain other things.

Drinking or smoking is catastrophic for health, no matter what quantity of alcohol you consume, you will reach a stage where you will be unable to fathom the reality and thus you will end up in danger. India is not a westernized nation, and no, alcohol cannot be a part of anybody's lifestyle here.

Homosexuality is queer, it is unnatural, it defies the law of nature and people who are homosexuals are under some bad influence. They all are high on something and don't actually know what they are doing, they should be treated.

One should not be married outside of one's own religion, it will only add to the population of the other religion. Also, we have a bias towards certain religions, we

exactly don't know what is wrong, but because we've been hearing it for ages, so it must be really wrong to marry someone of a different religion.

People can kill each other fighting once they are married, but they shouldn't get divorced, because what will the world say about them. The world which knows exactly nothing about what is happening between the two married individuals is entitled to have an opinion but the people concerned are not.

11

Russian taboo

Don't Show Up Empty Handed

If you're asked to join on a dinner, or even stop by for a visit, don't show up without anything to offer in return. It's not always most important what you do bring, but moreso what you don't. Bringing some chocolates, flowers (no even-numbered flowers, please), or even a toy for the kid is a better idea than to have no idea.

In Russia, hosts usually prepare for their company by offering their best prepared meals and special foods they normally wouldn't splurge on themselves. If you show up with nothing, it's a sign that you haven't a care for the hospitality in the first place.

Don't Forget to Take Your Shoes Off

This rule applies to both Russian and Asian cultures. In many Russian apartments, there are many rugs, on the floors and even the walls (quite an interesting tradition). Some may be quite nice – like Persian rugs and intricate designs, and often aren't the simple type that you just vacuum up to clean. This tradition has been going on for centuries, and hosts usually offer tapochki (slippers). At nice parties, some women may bring an extra pair of heels or shoes for inside use.

Never Whistle While Indoors

Did You Just Hear That? Oh, yeah, *that*. Sounded like bad luck. Superstitions say that it could lead to financial ruin, poverty, or just another invasion of cockroaches.

When Getting Acquainted Never Sit at the Corner of a Dinner Table

Forever Alone – Strangely I learned this one the hard way. It is said that the one who chooses a seat at the corner of a table is destined to never get married. For certain, they will never find their lover. This is mostly directed towards younger women, and some traditions say you won't get married for 7 years. So most of the time kids don't get scolded for this one.

Don't Ruin the Toast...

Before you make a special toast with your evening meal or perhaps just a casual blessing of vodka, keep in mind the proper toasts. The rules to Russian toasts are quite diverse, especially among nations of the former Eastern bloc.

I recall variations and traditions of toasting and drinking across Georgia, Moldova, Poland, Ukraine, and Russia that were in many ways similar but in some key ways different. If there was a Georgian present, you always knew, because after one man gave a toast, the second Georgian would be ready to toast. Until the next man, and on and on.

But "Na Zdorov'ye", literally meaning, For Your Health, is a Polish toast. Some suggest "Za zdoro v'ye" "Zah Vas", which means, "To You"

Keep the Empty Bottles off

Once vodka is finished, it's a rule that the bottle should be placed on the ground (if in the company as a guest, or one's home) as another is introduced. Russians are quite superstitious, and to leave an empty bottle on the table can irk some.

Never Take the Last Shirt

A funny Russian phrase begins with, Никогда отдать последнюю рубашку (nee-cog-dah ot-dat pos-led-nuyu rybashku) – Do not take back the last t-shirt. To put it in simpler terms – no matter of what expense you have for yourself, never be the one that takes the last. Always give back, and keep giving.

While living in Russia and meeting locals and their friends or families, I noticed some people who otherwise did not have much, were politely inclined to give what they felt was able to be given. The special bottle of the families' wines produced and made in their own Moldovan or Georgian homes, for instance, were the proper and chosen drinks for a common meal with guests. And while Moldovans and Georgians are different, some of the traditions I saw were quite similar.

This is not limited to common accommodations and drinks, but also photos, and other decorations you may find intriguing in one's home. Don't simply take something just because it is offered – some Russkies may offer something not to get rid of it, but out of simply a respectful and caring act.

Unless if you're into taking all that you can like some traveling gypsy, have some respect for the cultural norms, and understand that you can always refuse the first few times, even when your friends may insist. Personally, I only took gifts that had a strong memorable or shared aspect between the people I came to know, and the time we shared together. Likewise, I tried to give back anything that I could; as it is always nice to return this favor.

Never Lick The Food Off of a Knife.

Apparently it is unacceptable to lick any food or "remainders" off of a trusty utensil. It's considered rude and a sign of cruelty. Why would you lick the knife you used to tear through your food? Are you a savage? Such is a lesson learned in Novgorod…

Informal Dress Codes Are Not So Usual

Russians are known to dress quite nice, for a variety of occasions. A casual neighborhood, city park walk or even a meal with friends. Nice dresses and heels, suits or ties, it's common to see others' dressing their best as a sign of respect. I personally liked this a lot about Russian culture. In Moscow, I once saw a young teenager no older than 14 walk past me in a fully tailored suit in a mall on a Tuesday afternoon. I was a little surprised.

Dinner parties, trips to the opera, ballet, or even a theater – dress nicely, and expect others to do so too. Dining out is often considered a nice occasion, so the ripped jeans and Pearl Jam t-shirts can stay at home. Even if the venue is not so formal, it's a good idea to be prepared.

Going Dutch is Not Expected

This is where Russkies and some Westerners have some differences – while we live in different and changing times , the tradition of covering a meal and evening with a female is generally upheld. If you ask a nice lady out for diner, I wouldn't expect her to pay for the meal or anywhere else you decide to go. Some may offer to split the bill, but I wouldn't count on it. Hell, some of them may not even bring their rubles with them for such an occasion. If you expect to see her again, it's a safe bet that you should be ready to foot the bill like a gentleman.

Don't Smile Profusely

Maybe the hardest thing in Russia wasn't just learning the language and it's different parts. It was hard not to be stared at, to be *stared down*, rather by people. While riding the metro it isn't hard to be noticed as a foreigner. It's the little things you do. But one little thing that isn't widely accepted is to smile for no reason.

Russians have a saying, "To smile with no reason, is a sign of a fool." And that's a strong use of the word "fool". In college a Russian professor once told me, "It's not so common and maybe taken as a sign of being drunk or mentally ill." Her words, not mine.

Don't Expect A Lady to Carry

If you're accustomed to all things that are politically correct, double think it for a second. That lady carrying her luggage down the metro steps, or the lady at the airport getting ready to get her bags ready for her departure – always be there to lend a hand. It's polite, and as a man you are expected to be the one that assists in such a situation. You will see this even when getting in a taxi – the drivers will commonly be the ones that assist in the luggage. Such is a lesson in everyday life – lend a helping hand.

Never Disrespect Invalids

When you board a bus, or the city metro, you'll first notice that younger people will always be ready to lend a seat to the elderly, women, and children. This is a common norm you will run into everywhere, and may not always be the case in some countries. While some may be offended in some countries being offered this privilege, it's a sign of respect in Russia, and especially when elderly or pregnant women are standing there waiting for a seat it's downright rude.

Never Crack a Joke about One's Family

Though a lot of jokes you may hear in Russia and CIS, or perhaps even in many non-American countries may not be the most politically correct- you still should abide by a common rule. Never, ever, joke of the family members.

Growing up, I heard a plethora of "your momma" jokes, and while those jokes aren't the type we often hear later on in life, it's the same idea. The jokes surrounding others' family members are generally taboo to make, and to be quite honest – risky. You can crack a joke on ethnicity, appearance, or gender based jokes, but if you insult another's mother and father, it may not come across as a joke at all.

An Empty Purse is a Horrible Gift

Giving an empty purse as a gift is yet another superstition. Why is it empty? Do you wish financial hardship and poverty on your lover? Are you single again? Well to be fair, it applies to any money holding object one could thrown in as a gift.

Bodily Functions Are Frowned Upon
It is incredibly impolite, and you should not expect any kind of pride associated with such things. Burping loudly is not a game changing display of authority or humor. So if it happens, don't make a big deal out of it. Some say not to even apologize, but to simply ignore it. It's not of the most epic impressions you would want to make, so keep it in mind.

Never Show the Soles of Your Feet
This is common in many countries, but particularly it's another thing they say you shouldn't do in Russia. While on the metro once, I saw the angry looks of a few glances towards a foreign firmed of mine sitting across from me. She sat there texting, with her legs crossed – one over the other and her soles in the direction of the person sitting next to her. Shoe's aren't though to be the cleanest things one can point in the direct vicinity of another person, especially a stranger.

Don't Go for Shock Value
Despite what many Western journalists portrayed as an act of protest, the infamous *Pussy Riot* "protest" in the Cathedral of the Sacred heart was less impressive to the Russians I spoke with. Russians explained to me the history of this church – a long symbol of Orthodox and Christian faith in Russian history – which was even destroyed by the Soviets and turned into a pool. Following the collapse of the USSR, Russians contributed to charity and funded what they had left to rebuild this monument. A lot of those who I spoke with were not impressed at all, or supportive of Pussy Riot. "If they wanted to protest, why would they have chosen such a place?" I guess the line between controversy and shock value hit it off pretty well here.

Never Shake a Hand Through a Doorway
Russian's are very superstitious, so superstitious in fact, it ties into getting acquainted. It is considered rude to shake hands with your gloves on – so take your gloves off before any proper interaction occurs. Additionally, shaking ones hand at

the door is considered back luck. So make sure to take your gloves off, and save the hand shaking for indoors. And even then you have to take off your snow boots or else you'll come across like a total ass.

(http://trevorabroad.com/russian-taboo.html)

www.ingramcontent.com/pod-product-compliance
Lightning Source LLC
Chambersburg PA
CBHW050903290526
45792CB00002B/691